P9-ELP-073

A HISTORY OF BRITAIN

PAPERBIRD

Acknowledgments:

The publishers would like to acknowledge the use of additional illustrative material as follows: Colchester and Essex Museum, cover, pages 15, 44; English Heritage, cover, pages 21, 26; Fitzwilliam Museum, cover, page 9 (right); Fortean Picture Library, pages 28, 30; Robert Harding, cover, pages 33, 34 (inset), 36, 37; Hunting Aerofilms, page 51 (top); Mansell Collection, page 40; Museum of London, pages 23, 51 (bottom); National Museum of Wales, pages 9 (left), 10; National Trust, Tewkesbury, pages 34, 47; Pimperne House, Butser Ancient Farm Project Trust, page 7; Society of Antiquaries of London, page 20; Trustees of the British Museum, pages 10 (inset), 13, 19; Tyne and Wear Museum Service, page 51; Warburg Institute © University of London, pages 45, 51 (bottom); Anne Matthews, line drawing on page 45; John Dillow, illustration on page 52 (top) and illustration on page 53.

Designed by Gavin Young.

British Library Cataloguing in Publication Data

Wood, Tim
    The Romans
    1. Roman Empire. Civilization
    I. Title   II. Dennis, Peter   III. Series
    937
    ISBN 1-85543-006-1

Published by Ladybird Books Ltd Loughborough Leicestershire UK
Ladybird Books Inc Auburn Maine 04210 USA
Paperbird is an imprint of Ladybird Books Ltd
© LADYBIRD BOOKS LTD MCMLXXXIX

Printed in England

Contents

THE
ROMANS

by TIM WOOD

illustrations by PETER DENNIS

Series Consultants: School of History
University of Bristol

Paperbird

The Romans

This book covers a period of over four hundred and fifty years. During this time, the Iron Age Britons were conquered by the Romans. Britain became part of the mighty Roman Empire, which stretched from what is now north of England to the Red Sea. Many Britons were forced to accept the Roman way of life.

Roman Britain – time chart

Date	What happened
55 BC	Roman fleet appears off British coast
54 BC	Julius Caesar lands in Britain
0	
AD 43	Claudius invades Britain with his general, Aulus Plautus. Most of England conquered in four years. The legionaries begin to build fortresses. Caratacus defeated in Wales and taken prisoner
	Suetonius becomes Governor of Britain and attacks the Druids on Anglesey
AD 60	The Iceni tribe, led by Boudicca, revolts, burns London, and is then defeated.
	The Brigantes tribe is conquered
	Wales is conquered and many legionary forts built there
	Agricola becomes Governor of Britain and marches into Scotland (Caledonia) defeating the Caledonians at the battle of Mons Graupius
	Roman towns built at Lincoln and Gloucester
AD 100	Scotland abandoned
AD 122	The Emperor Hadrian visits Britain
	Hadrian's wall is begun

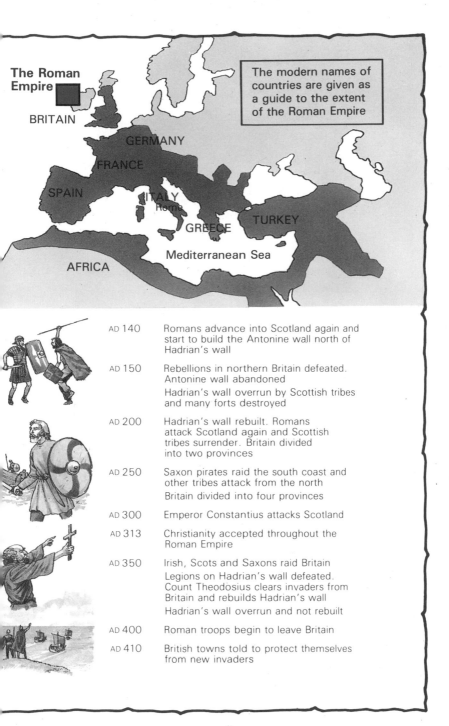

The Roman Empire

BRITAIN

The modern names of countries are given as a guide to the extent of the Roman Empire

GERMANY

FRANCE

SPAIN

ITALY
Rome

GREECE

TURKEY

Mediterranean Sea

AFRICA

AD 140	Romans advance into Scotland again and start to build the Antonine wall north of Hadrian's wall
AD 150	Rebellions in northern Britain defeated. Antonine wall abandoned
	Hadrian's wall overrun by Scottish tribes and many forts destroyed
AD 200	Hadrian's wall rebuilt. Romans attack Scotland again and Scottish tribes surrender. Britain divided into two provinces
AD 250	Saxon pirates raid the south coast and other tribes attack from the north
	Britain divided into four provinces
AD 300	Emperor Constantius attacks Scotland
AD 313	Christianity accepted throughout the Roman Empire
AD 350	Irish, Scots and Saxons raid Britain
	Legions on Hadrian's wall defeated. Count Theodosius clears invaders from Britain and rebuilds Hadrian's wall
	Hadrian's wall overrun and not rebuilt
AD 400	Roman troops begin to leave Britain
AD 410	British towns told to protect themselves from new invaders

Britain before the Roman invasion

About two thousand seven hundred years ago, people called *Celts* came to Britain from Europe. Gradually, they mixed in with the people who were already there. All those living in Britain became known as Britons. They were divided into groups called tribes.

A British settlement about 2,200 years ago

The cooking fire was kept going all the time

making baskets

grinding corn using a *quern*

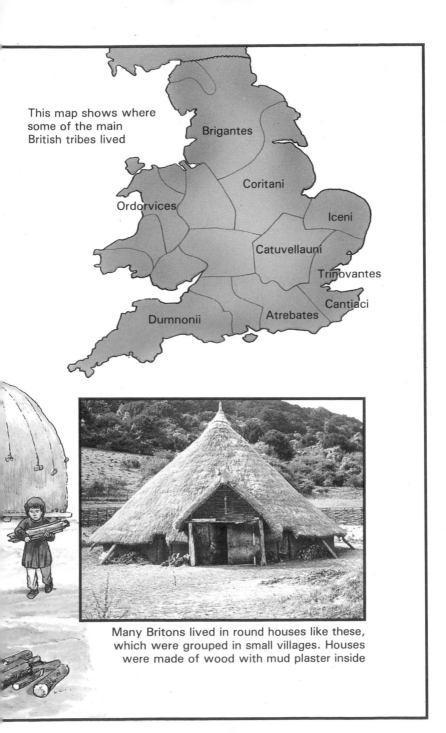

This map shows where some of the main British tribes lived

Brigantes

Coritani

Ordorvices

Iceni

Catuvellauni

Trinovantes

Cantiaci

Dumnonii

Atrebates

Many Britons lived in round houses like these, which were grouped in small villages. Houses were made of wood with mud plaster inside

British towns before the Romans

The Celts brought with them the skill of making iron tools and weapons. They built towns, which became trading centres.

Iron Age towns were dirty and smelly

Prisoners captured in war were sold as slaves

People came to the towns to swap food and animals from their farms for pottery, jewellery, silver and iron goods. Some British tribes already traded with the Roman Empire, which covered most of Europe. They sold lead, gold, tin, wheat, slaves, cattle, hunting dogs and pearls to the Romans.

a coin maker

Slaves were chained with iron collars like this

A British coin. Coins were first used in Britain about 2,150 years ago

Nobles and Druids

The leaders of the British tribes were called nobles. They drove chariots into battle while ordinary warriors fought on foot with spears and swords. Many painted or tattooed themselves with a blue dye called woad.

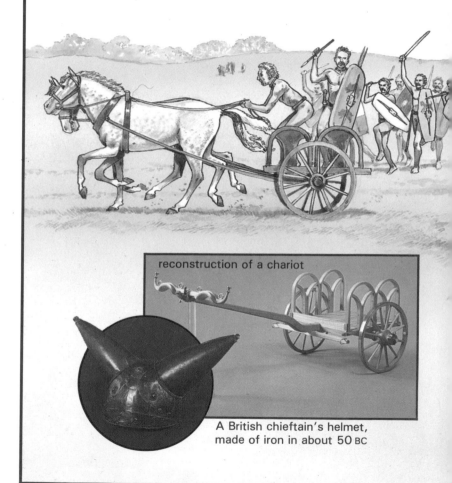

reconstruction of a chariot

A British chieftain's helmet, made of iron in about 50 BC

It is thought that the *Druids*, or priests, had great power. Little is known of their religion except that they believed in many gods and they may have sacrificed humans. They had fled to Britain from Europe when the Romans had tried to stamp out their cruel religion.

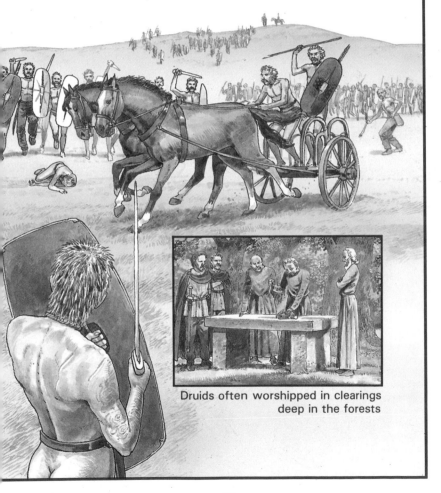

Druids often worshipped in clearings deep in the forests

The Romans attack Britain, 55 BC

On a late summer morning in 55 BC, a Roman fleet appeared off the British coast near Dover. Consul Julius Caesar had brought an army of 10,000 men to see if Britain was worth invading. He also wanted to punish those British tribes who had been helping the Celts in Europe in their fight against the Romans.

At first the Romans were afraid of the thousands of British warriors waiting to fight them on the beach. It was not until the standard bearer of the 10th legion jumped into the water that the rest of the Roman soldiers followed.

The Britons fought desperately, but they were no match for the well trained Romans, and soon fled.

After his victory, Caesar left Britain. He returned with another army in the following year but left shortly after. The Romans did not return to Britain for ninety seven years.

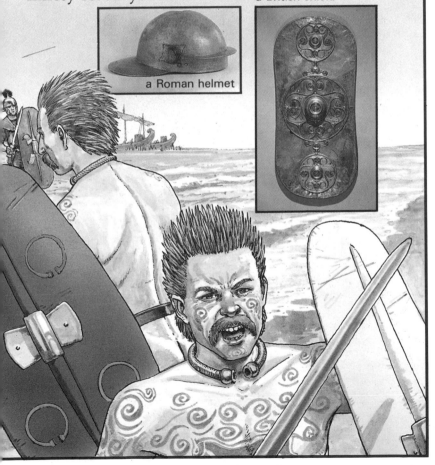

a British shield

a Roman helmet

Conquest, AD 43 – AD 60

In AD 43, the Roman Emperor, Claudius, decided to make Britain part of the Roman Empire. An army of 40,000 Roman soldiers landed at Richborough in Kent. This time the Romans had come to stay.

Roman soldiers swam across the water in their armour to capture the island of Anglesey, the centre of the Druid religion

Gloucester

The chief enemy of Rome, Caratacus, King of the Catuvellauni, fought the Romans in Wales. But he was betrayed by the Queen of the Brigantes, captured and sent to Rome as a slave

The Roman army swept the Britons aside and marched deep into the countryside. They made alliances with some tribes and conquered others, one by one. Slowly, they drove their enemies into the mountains of Wales and Scotland.

The Romans did not invade Scotland until AD 84. Although they won some battles they could not conquer Scotland

Hadrian's wall

York

Chester

Wherever they went, the Romans built roads and forts to control the Britons

Emperor Claudius

The Roman army

The Roman soldiers who invaded Britain were part of the best army in the world. They were better trained and armed than the wild Britons.

The Roman army was divided into *legions*, each one containing roughly 5,000 *legionaries* who signed up for twenty five years. Each legionary was highly trained with daily sword practice and marching. Legionaries were also trained to build roads, bridges, forts and *siege-engines*.

A legionary wore heavy armour and had a large shield for protection. He carried two javelins and a short, sharp sword. Each legionary took food, cooking gear, an axe and two sharp stakes to help to build a wall round the camp at night.

A Roman legionary with his armour and equipment

The Roman army also contained many auxiliaries. These were soldiers from conquered tribes all over the Roman Empire.

Some auxiliaries had special skills:

Archers – many came from Syria. The Romans also used mounted archers

Slingers – many came from the Balearic Islands in the Mediterranean Sea

The *cavalry* was used for scouting and carrying messages. They also chased fleeing enemy soldiers during battles

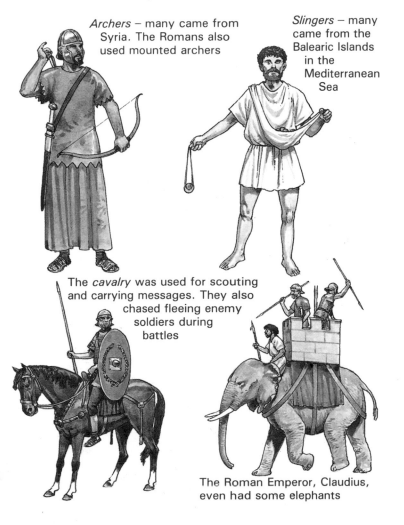

The Roman Emperor, Claudius, even had some elephants

Battle

Legionaries were taught to fight in different formations. This usually gave them an advantage over their enemies who were not so well organised. In battle the whole army could fight as one man or split into smaller groups. Trumpets were used to give the signals.

cohort (about 480 soldiers)
There were 10 cohorts in a legion

A standard bearer. Each legion had its own standard called an *eagle*

An experienced officer called a *centurion* was in charge of a century

century (about 80 soldiers) There were 6 centuries in a cohort

a Roman sword

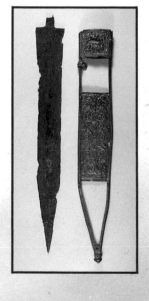

British hill forts

The British tribes had built many hill forts. The Romans could not conquer Britain until they had captured these strongholds.

wooden walls

ditch

There were different kinds of hill forts. Many had several ditches and walls round the hill top. A maze sometimes hid the main gate.

The tribe lived in huts built inside the walls. They brought their animals into the enclosure for safety when the fort was attacked.

The body of this Briton was found at Maiden Castle in Dorset. A ballista bolt had passed through his body and lodged in his spine

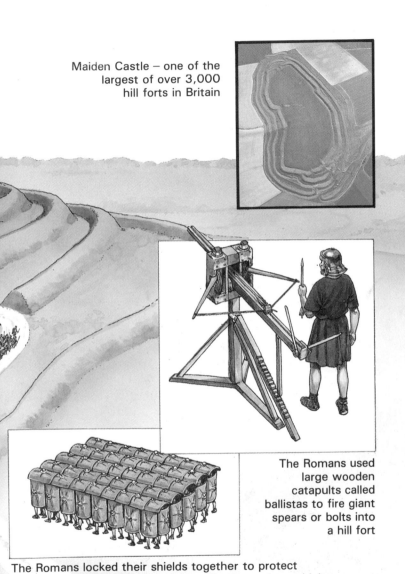

Maiden Castle – one of the
largest of over 3,000
hill forts in Britain

The Romans used
large wooden
catapults called
ballistas to fire giant
spears or bolts into
a hill fort

The Romans locked their shields together to protect
themselves from rocks and spears. The formation, which
looked like a hard shell, was called a 'tortoise'

Boudicca's revolt, AD 60

The fighting continued for almost twenty years after the Roman invasion. The Romans won many victories and it seemed as though nothing could stop them from ruling the whole country.

Then, in AD 60, the Iceni tribe led by their queen, Boudicca, revolted.

Boudicca's army burned the Roman cities of Colchester...

St Albans...

and London

They destroyed an entire legion

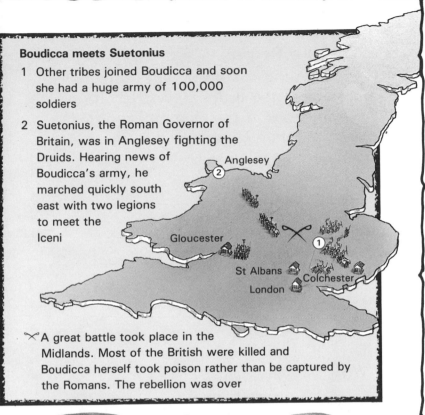

Boudicca meets Suetonius

1. Other tribes joined Boudicca and soon she had a huge army of 100,000 soldiers

2. Suetonius, the Roman Governor of Britain, was in Anglesey fighting the Druids. Hearing news of Boudicca's army, he marched quickly south east with two legions to meet the Iceni

Anglesey ②

Gloucester

St Albans
London
Colchester

①

✕ A great battle took place in the Midlands. Most of the British were killed and Boudicca herself took poison rather than be captured by the Romans. The rebellion was over

These skulls, found in a London stream bed, may have belonged to three of Boudicca's victims

The new Britons

After Boudicca's revolt, the Romans brought a new order to Britain. It became part of the Roman Empire and more Romans began to settle there. Latin became the main language for administration. Everyone had to obey

The Romans built towns and cities which became centres of trade. Some Roman Britons grew wealthy by selling goods to the Romans.

Roman governors were sent to rule Britain. The new laws brought peace although Roman Britons now had to pay taxes to Rome.

Roman laws and follow the Roman way of life. Soon it was hard to tell who had been born in Britain and who was a foreigner. Britons became 'Roman Britons'.

British nobles were trained to rule their tribes in the Roman way. This brought peace and riches to many, although some Britons who continued to fight against their new rulers were captured and became slaves. The Roman army built good roads so the legions could march quickly to any part of the country to keep the peace.

Hadrian's wall

The Romans built forts in Wales and in the north of England to protect their land. The fierce, unconquered tribes hiding in the mountains and valleys of Scotland raided northern England again and again.

The Emperor Hadrian decided to build a wall right across the country from Wallsend in Tyne and Wear to Bowness in Cumbria, to control them.

milecastle

Hadrian's wall was finished in AD 128. The illustration shows what it may have looked like about AD 150 and the photograph shows the wall as it is today

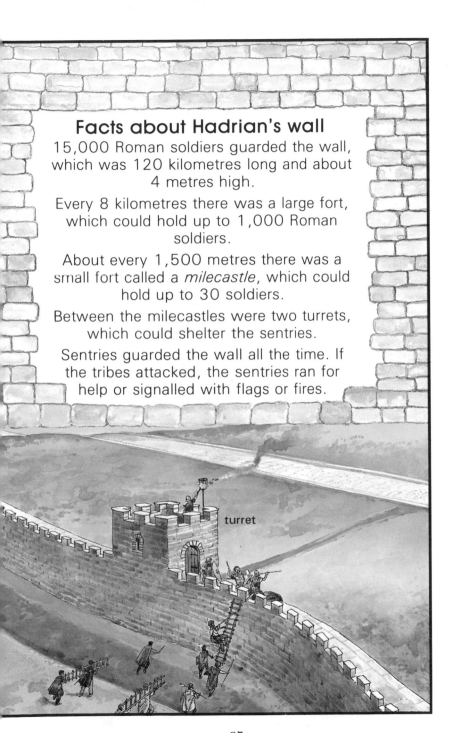

Facts about Hadrian's wall

15,000 Roman soldiers guarded the wall, which was 120 kilometres long and about 4 metres high.

Every 8 kilometres there was a large fort, which could hold up to 1,000 Roman soldiers.

About every 1,500 metres there was a small fort called a *milecastle*, which could hold up to 30 soldiers.

Between the milecastles were two turrets, which could shelter the sentries.

Sentries guarded the wall all the time. If the tribes attacked, the sentries ran for help or signalled with flags or fires.

turret

Roman roads

The Romans built many roads. The legionaries did all the work, digging out the trenches, cutting the stones to shape, and laying them. A curved surface and ditches at the side made sure that the rain ran off the road and did not wash the stones away.

Remains of a Roman road in Yorkshire

milestone

Roman surveyors used an instrument called a *groma*. Strings with weights were hung from a wooden frame so that the surveyor could get a straight line by looking through them. Where trees or hills were in the way, the surveyors built fires in a straight line and used the smoke to mark the route.

chalk, sand and broken brick

ditch

surface made from shaped, flat stones or gravel

strong base of shaped stones

chalk and sand

Roman towns

From about AD 150 onwards, the Romans built walls round their towns to keep them safe from attack.

Strongly built towns helped to keep peace and showed the Roman Britons how good Roman life could be.

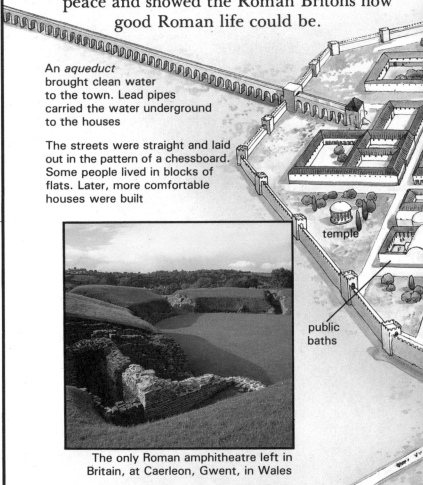

An *aqueduct* brought clean water to the town. Lead pipes carried the water underground to the houses

The streets were straight and laid out in the pattern of a chessboard. Some people lived in blocks of flats. Later, more comfortable houses were built

temple

public baths

The only Roman amphitheatre left in Britain, at Caerleon, Gwent, in Wales

People came to the towns to buy and sell goods, to pay their taxes and to enjoy themselves.

This illustration is based on the Roman town of Silchester, Hampshire

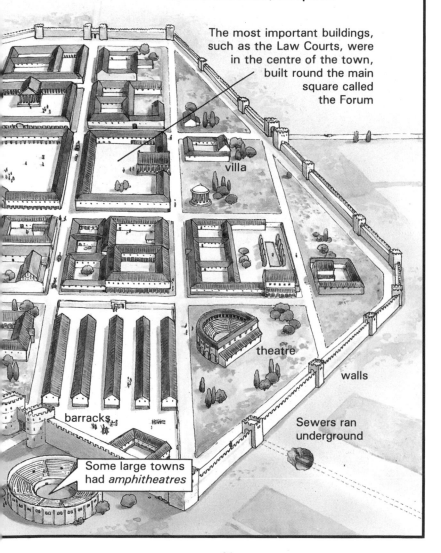

The most important buildings, such as the Law Courts, were in the centre of the town, built round the main square called the Forum

villa

theatre

walls

barracks

Sewers ran underground

Some large towns had *amphitheatres*

The baths

Romans went to the baths to keep clean, relax, meet their friends and to exercise. Women and men bathed at separate times of the day.

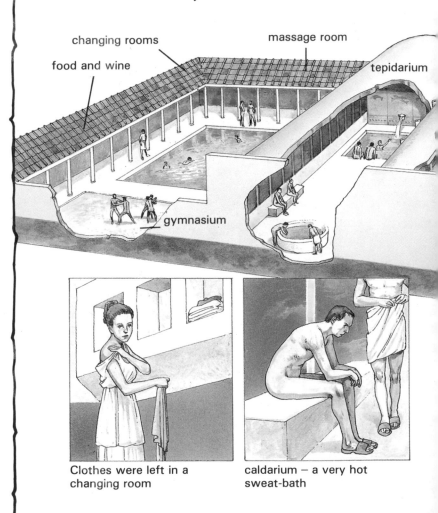

changing rooms

food and wine

massage room

tepidarium

gymnasium

Clothes were left in a changing room

caldarium – a very hot sweat-bath

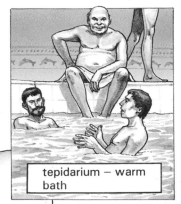
tepidarium – warm bath

Food and wine were sold

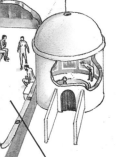
caldarium

The Roman baths at Bath

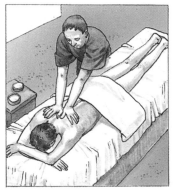
massage room

gymnasium – for exercise

In the house

Rich Romans and Roman Britons lived in the towns, in fine houses which were built in the Roman style.

plastered walls

The floors were covered with *mosaics* – pictures or patterns made from tiny pieces of coloured marble stuck in cement

The remains of the central heating system at Chedworth Villa, Gloucester

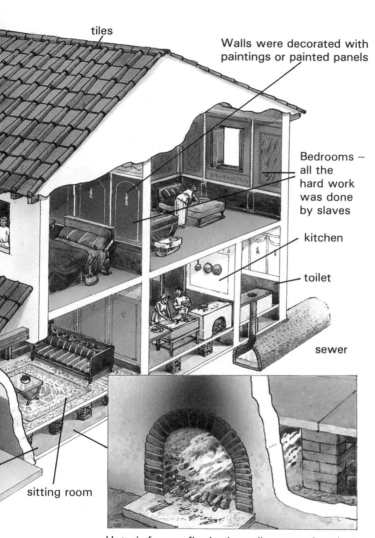

tiles

Walls were decorated with paintings or painted panels

Bedrooms —
all the
hard work
was done
by slaves

kitchen

toilet

sewer

sitting room

Hot air from a fire in the cellar passed under the floor and up the walls to heat the house. This central heating system was called a *hypocaust*

Food in a rich household

The kitchen stove was an open hearth filled with *charcoal*. Most of the cooking pots were made of pottery although some were iron. The burning charcoal must have made the kitchen very hot for the slaves who were getting the food ready.

Roman spoons

open hearth

quern

amphora for holding olive oil

The kitchen slaves washed the vegetables and herbs in a stone sink. Baking was very difficult because there was no oven in the house, so bread, cakes and puddings were usually bought from a baker.

Roman kitchen objects

Spices were pounded with a pestle and mortar

turnips

snails fattening in milk

carrots

peas

A feast

Most people were too poor to buy fish or meat. They ate mainly porridge, green vegetables and pancakes, washed down with watered wine.

This is what a feast in a rich Roman household may have looked like

First course

raw vegetables

eggs

shellfish

stuffed dormice

Second course

boiled meat

roast meat

doves

chicken

pork

roast boar

Guests who were invited to a feast in a rich person's house lay on couches and ate with their fingers. Slaves cut up the meat for them, served out the food and brought round bowls of water so that the guests could wash their hands between courses. Poets and musicians provided entertainment.

slave carving meat

oil lamp

Guests washed their hands between courses

pipes

stringed instrument called a cithara

Third course

fruit

honey cakes

spiced loaf

stuffed dates

What people wore

Women wore sleeveless tunics made from linen or cotton, or, if they were very rich, silk. They wore coloured shawls over their tunics and as much jewellery as they could afford.

Hairstyles were often quite elaborate

shawl

Female slaves wore simple tunics

Most Romans wore boots or sandals

Men wore togas – loose robes made from the best wool if they were rich, or from coarse cloth if they were poor. Togas could be any colour but officials usually wore white togas decorated with a coloured stripe to show that the wearer was an important person.

putting on a toga

1

tunic

2

3

toga

4

the toga of a Roman citizen

Slaves wore simple tunics made of coarse cloth or felt

School

Only the children of rich parents went to school, starting at about the age of seven. They left primary school at the age of twelve. Boys went on to secondary school but girls, who were allowed to marry at the age of twelve, usually stopped going to school or had a home tutor.

The lessons were dull, with lots of copying and learning by heart. Schoolmasters were very strict and some beat their pupils.

Maths was taught with an *abacus*

Pupils wrote on wooden boards spread with wax. They wrote in the wax with the point of a bronze or wooden *stylus* and rubbed out mistakes with the flattened end. The wax was smoothed and used many times

The school day began at dawn and lasted about six hours, with a mid-day break for the pupils to eat their picnic lunch. As the Romans had no weekends, the pupils had to work for seven days before they had a day off for market day.

Schools were very small, just one teacher with a class of ten pupils. Young children learned reading, writing and maths. Older children learned grammar, history, geography and how to speak well in public.

Religion

The Romans brought their own religion to Britain. They worshipped many gods and goddesses in the new temples that they built. There was no special day for worship, so people went to the temple whenever they wanted and spoke to the god's statue to give thanks or to ask a favour.

Many Roman emperors were worshipped as gods after they died. This is a model of the temple of Claudius which was built at Colchester, Essex, about AD 54

People also worshipped at home. Each home had its own household gods. Every day the family said prayers, and left food and salt in front of a little shrine.

A statue of Mercury who was the messenger of the gods

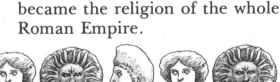

This carving shows animals being taken for *sacrifice* to a household god. These sacrifices took place on important feast days

Soon after the Roman invasion of Britain, Christianity began to spread throughout the Roman Empire. Many emperors tried to stop it, but they failed. In AD 313, Christianity became the religion of the whole Roman Empire.

The villa

Many rich Romans owned a villa in the country. This was both a holiday home and a working farm, surrounded by fields and gardens. The owner was often away, either on business or working at his job in a nearby town. When he was not there, a manager ran the farm and organised the slaves.

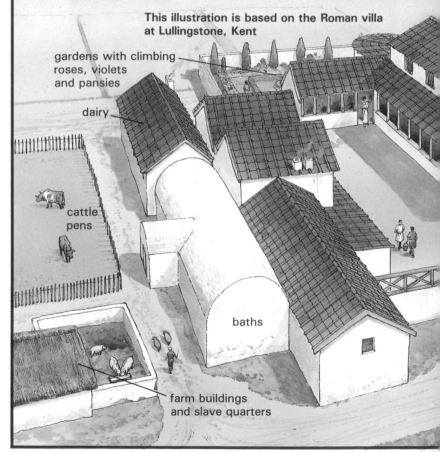

This illustration is based on the Roman villa at Lullingstone, Kent

gardens with climbing roses, violets and pansies

dairy

cattle pens

baths

farm buildings and slave quarters

Excavations on the site of the Roman villa at Chedworth, Gloucester

tannery for turning cattle hides into leather

main house

Grain was dried and stored in a granary

owner inspecting the farm with his manager

A good water supply was important

The Romans leave Britain

The Romans ruled Britain for over three hundred and fifty years. For some Roman Britons this was a time of peace and plenty, but many soldiers were needed to keep Britain safe. After AD 250, this task became harder.

Raiders from Scotland and Ireland began to make attacks on Britain.

Saxon pirates made raids across the North Sea. The Roman forts on the south and east coasts could not keep them out.

The Roman Empire itself was being attacked by barbarians. Gradually legions left Britain to defend other parts of the Empire. In AD 411, no more pay was sent from Rome and few Roman soldiers stayed after that.

The Britons were left to protect themselves from the new invaders. With the Romans gone there was no strong leader to rule the whole country and gradually the Roman way of life disappeared. Many people returned to the countryside and allowed the towns to fall into ruins.

ROMANS 700BC – AD383	SAXONS AND NORMANS 383 – 1272	 MIDDLE AGES 1272 – 1485	TUDORS 1485 – 1603
1083 yrs	889 yrs	213 yrs	118 yrs

TIMELINE GUIDE TO *A HISTORY OF BRITAIN*

How we know

The events in this book happened over fifteen hundred years ago – so how do we know about them?

Historians use EVIDENCE, rather like detectives do, to piece a story together.

Some BOOKS describing Roman Britain have survived to this day. One of the best known Roman writers is Julius Caesar, who wrote a book called *Conquest of Gaul* in which he described his invasion of Britain. Other Roman historians wrote about Britain. One, Cornelius Tacitus, was son in law to Agricola, one of the Roman governors of Britain. Naturally enough his account of Agricola's rule was rather flattering!

Julius Caesar

There are still a lot of BUILDINGS which have survived as ruins to this day.

STUARTS 1603 – 1714	GEORGIANS 1714 – 1830	VICTORIANS 1830 – 1901	MODERN TIMES 1901 – 1945

111 yrs	116 yrs	71 yrs	44 yrs

The remains of the Roman theatre at Verulamium – St Albans

Archaeologists have *excavated* many Roman sites. Often they have found these by looking at PHOTOGRAPHS taken from the air.

OBJECTS found by archaeologists are often stored in museums. Most of the objects are made of metal, stone or pottery. We have fewer objects made from cloth or wood

because they rot easily. There is a list of museums and buildings to visit on page 56.

Some of the old Roman objects seem strange to us. What do you think these are? You will find the answer on page 56.

The Roman legacy

It is important to remember that the Romans brought many good things to Britain. They improved trade and the quality of life for many Britons.

Roman towns showed the Britons that life could be comfortable and pleasant.

Roman laws meant that arguments could be settled peacefully. Some of our modern laws are based on Roman laws.

The Romans brought milestones to Britain. This drawing shows a stone milestone from Hadrian's reign. Originally it would have stood 2-3 metres high. The letters 'MPIIII' mean 'four miles from...'

Other things the Romans brought to Britain

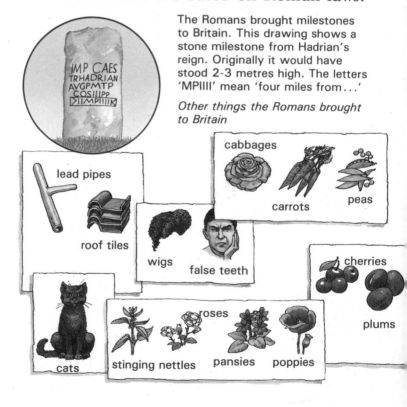

lead pipes

roof tiles

cabbages

carrots

peas

wigs

false teeth

cherries

plums

cats

stinging nettles

roses

pansies

poppies

Many of our words are based on Latin words. The Romans gave us the names of all our months

JANUARY — named after the Roman god JANUS. He could look both ways at once because he had two faces, and was the god of gateways

JANUS

FEBRUARY — named after the Roman festival of FEBRUA

MARCH — named after MARS, the Roman war god

APRIL — from the Latin word APERIRE meaning 'to open' – because of the unfolding of buds and blossom in spring

MARS

MAY — named after MAIA, the Roman mother goddess

JUNE — named after JUNO, wife of Jupiter, King of the Roman gods

JULY — named after JULIUS Caesar, who decided that the year should begin in January. Until then it had begun in March

JUNO

AUGUST — named after the Roman Emperor AUGUSTUS

SEPTEMBER — from the Latin word SEPTEM, meaning 'seven'. It was originally the seventh month of the year

OCTOBER — from the Latin word OCTO, meaning 'eight'. It was originally the eighth month of the year

JULIUS CAESAR

NOVEMBER — from the Latin word NOVEM, meaning 'nine'. It was originally the ninth month of the year

DECEMBER — from the Latin word DECEM, meaning 'ten'. It was originally the tenth month of the year

AUGUSTUS

Glossary

abacus: a frame holding beads for counting

aqueduct: a system of pipes and structures used to carry water from its source to the towns

amphitheatre: a circular or oval open-air theatre used for gladiator and animal fights

amphora: a tall pottery oil jar

archaeologist: someone who digs up and studies ancient remains

archer: a bowman

cavalry: soldiers who fought on horseback

Celts: Iron Age tribes from Europe

centurion: an officer in charge of a century

century: a group of legionaries, about 80 soldiers

charcoal: baked wood which burns at a high temperature

cohort: a group of legionaries, about 480 soldiers

Druid: a priest

eagle: the standard of a legion. It was a bronze model of an eagle on a long staff

excavate: to dig up ancient remains

groma: an instrument used for surveying

hypocaust: underfloor hot-air central heating system

legion: a group of legionaries, about 5,000 soldiers

legionary: a member of a legion

milecastle: a Roman fort on Hadrian's wall

mosaic: a picture or pattern made of coloured tiles

quern: two round stones, one on top of the other for grinding corn

sacrifice: an offering made to the gods

siege-engine: a machine used to capture a castle

slinger: a soldier who hurled clay or lead bullets using a long leather thong called a sling

stylus: a pointed metal instrument used for scratching words in wax

Index

Some places you can visit to find out more about the Romans

MUSEUMS
British Museum, London
Caerleon Museum, Gwent
The Castle, Colchester, Essex
City and County Museum, Lincoln
Corinium Museum, Cirencester, Gloucestershire
Corstopitum Roman Fort, Corbridge, Northumberland
Fishbourne Roman Palace and Museum,
    near Chichester, Sussex
Housesteads, Hadrian's Wall Museum and Fort,
    Hexham, Northumberland
Jewry Wall Museum, Leicester
Museum of London, London
Roman Baths Museum, Bath
Verulamium Museum, St Albans

VILLAS, FORTS, etc
Bignor Villa, West Sussex
Burgh Castle, Great Yarmouth
Chesters Roman Fort, Chollerford, Northumberland
Chedworth Villa, Gloucestershire
Lullingstone Villa, Sevenoaks, Kent
Lunt Fort, Baginton, near Coventry
Maiden Castle, Dorset
Roman Army Museum, Greenhead, Northumberland
Roman Lighthouse, Dover
Roman Villa, Rockbourne, Fordingbridge, Hampshire
Verulamium Theatre, St Albans
Vindolanda Roman Fort, Bardon Mill, Northumberland
Wroxeter Roman Baths, Shropshire

The picture on page 51 shows an oil jar and scraper (called a strigil). These were used by Roman Britons in the baths. They rubbed the oil on their skin to bring the dirt to the surface and then used the strigil to scrape it off